HAUN͟TED ELY

Vivienne Doughty & Margaret Haynes

S.B. Publications

To Emily and Mark

First published in 1996 by S.B. Publications
c/o 19 Grove Road, Seaford, East Sussex BN25 1TP

Reprinted 1997

ISBN 1 85770 110 0

Typeset, printed and bound by MFP Design & Print, Longford Trading Estate,
Thomas Street, Stretford, Manchester M32 0JT; tel 0161–864 4540; fax 0161–866 9866.

Contents

Front Cover
> Infirmary Chapel archway, now entrance yard to the Chapter Office and
> back entrance of the Deanery.

Back Cover
> Infirmary Chapel archway looking out towards Firmary Lane.

Title Page
> Ely Deanery from the park with monastic buildings and the Cathedral in background.
> (note the open window of Elizabeth Goudge's former bedroom)

Acknowledgements

The authors are indebted to the following people.

Pamela Blakeman, Reg and Anita Brown, Alison Curtis-Smith and the staff of Oliver Cromwell House, The Dean of Ely, Barbara and Tim Eaton, Barbara and Tony Gipp, Malcolm Graham, Bill Green, Joan Griffin, Bunty Jones, Paul Loose, Chris and Peter Kerswell, The King's School Boarders, Kate Marshall, Canon Neil Munt, Connie May, Liz Nardone, Les Oakey, Jo and Andrew Odell-Rourke, Jill Peak, Graham and Margaret Peters, Christine Pownell, Tony Ransome, Mallyan Thompson, Christine Wall, and many others who wish to remain anonymous. Their stories and snippets of information have been the inspiration for this book.

Monastic map by courtesy of Ely Cathedral.

All photographs by Vivienne Doughty.

Introduction

After taking an amazing ghost tour of York in 1985, Blue Badge Tourist Guide Margaret Haynes was inspired to develop her own local ghost tour . The history of Ely is equally long and fascinating as that of York. St. Etheldreda founded a monastery here in 673 but nomadic tribes hunted and fished in the area long before that. When the Waitrose site was developed bronze age artifacts were found. Any place with a past is bound to have ghosts.

Margaret started with material she had already collected but began writing down scraps of information given to her by local people who came along on her tours. Gradually these scraps built up and merged into ghost stories that fitted with her knowledge of the history of the region. Soon there was far too much for an hour long tour and she could afford to become selective. Admirers urged her to write a book and eventually the idea lodged in her head. During extensive reading of ghost tales Margaret had never come across a single mention of an Ely sighting. A bookseller friend mentioned that visitors to the city were often disappointed to find no books about Ely ghosts. The problem was that although Margaret could talk thirteen to the dozen she didn't feel she had the technical knowledge to embark on writing a book. What she needed was *her very own ghost writer* and so she approached me. We were both Ely and East Anglia Blue Badge Guides and so shared an interest in the history of the area. Margaret's main interest was ghosts. Mine was writing about local history for magazines. It seemed a good combination. We found a publisher within the month. I did the writing. Margaret did the research. The ghosts didn't exist in a vacuum. They fitted in snugly with local history so the book became more a story of Ely's past than a list of its ghosts.

Damaris Vivienne Doughty

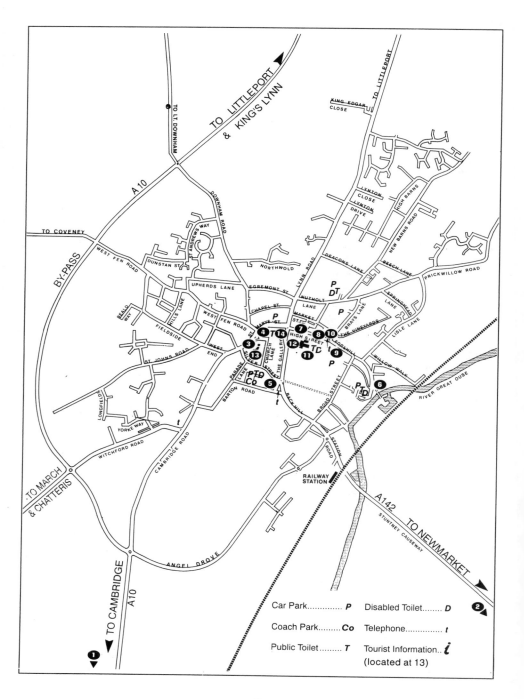

Car Park............. **P** Disabled Toilet........ **D**

Coach Park......... **Co** Telephone............... **t**

Public Toilet .... **T** Tourist Information.. **i**
(located at 13)

City of Ely Street Map

List of sites referred to in the book:

1. Black Shuck and A10 /Witchford Airfield

2. Stuntney Old Hall

3. Oliver Cromwell House, Tourist Information Centre

4. The Chantry on Palace Green

5. Medieval Cottages. Silver Street

6. Waterside Antiques

7. Steeple Gate

8. The North Range

9. Smiths the Cleaners

10. Peck's Ironmongers Shop

11. Firmary Lane
(The Deanery, The Black Hostelry, Powcher's Hall, Canonry House, Walsingham House (The Painted Chamber)

12. The Cathedral

13. Parade Lane / The Range

14. The Old Palace on Palace Green

1: Black Shuck

Black Shuck, the wild, pagan dog of the Saxons, has frequently been spotted around Cambridgeshire and East Anglia. His origin is obscure but the name is derived from the Anglo Saxon word 'soucca' meaning demon. According to legend this huge, shaggy creature frequents ancient tracks or sits guarding bridges and gateways, his great shining eyes glowing with red and yellow fire.

A statue of him on top of a lamp-post in Bungay, Suffolk, reminds inhabitants of the time in 1577 when ball lightning hit the church killing members of the congregation and damaging the building. Black Shuck got the blame. He is reputed to cause death within twelve months among the families of those who see him, so beware. In Arbury Road, Cambridge, he bounds along at great speed but slows down to howl and snarl at pedestrians. He has been spotted at Balsham with a monkey's face, at West Wratting, West Wickham and Devil's Dyke at Reach.

In the Ely area Black Shuck, crosses the Cambridge bound A10 between Braham Farm and the old Witchford aerodrome site towards dusk, causing chaos and fear among motorists. Braham Farm lies on the ancient footpath that used to lead from Angel Drove on the west side of Ely. Nearby is Bedwell Hay Farm, site of the Saxon settlement Cratendune. The land was given to Saxon Princess Etheldreda by her first husband Tondbert, prince of the South Girvii tribe and probable first ruler of the Isle. The monastery built by Etheldreda in 673 may have been on this site so a Saxon dog would feel comfortable here.

Albert Gipp used to see Black Shuck quite often when he was a lad before the last war. He lived with his family in a little cottage on the river bank at Prickwillow and used to watch the huge black hound bounding along the Lark bank in the direction of Ely.

Mr. and Mrs. C.E. Fuller saw him in Soham one evening in the late 1970's as they were driving past Downfield's mill on the A142. They had to pull up sharply to avoid the great black dog who ran across the road straight in front of them by the Cherry Tree pub. They watched anxiously for his arrival on the other side by the old footpath that leads towards Wicken but he had disappeared. At Wicken he 'pads noiselessly along Spinney Bank with his blood red eyes as large as saucers.'

Brandon Bank where Black Shuck has been sighted.

When Paul Loose was out exercising his dogs near Brandon Bank late at night he twice saw red eyes blinking at him in the darkness and a vague shape beyond. He moved to the Fens in March 1996 and didn't know about Black Shuck till he read *The Ely Standard* during May and learned of the legend. Could this be the solution to the puzzle of the mysterious Fen Tiger that has so often been sighted around this region? In April 1996 it was spotted in Newmarket early one morning down New Cheveley Road. It is said to be an escaped panther or black leopard but isn't it more likely to be the Saxon ghost dog?

A programme on Channel 4 in July '96 entitled ' Beast of the Fens ' claimed over 100 sightings in Cambridgeshire of a black cat like creature about 4ft in length with a flattened tiger like face. The programme came to no conclusion but the idea of the animal being a phantom was not mentioned. Ann Bradford, author of *Midland Ghosts and Hauntings*, says that 'ghosts of animals are usually bad news' but Ely can boast a friendly version of Black Shuck.

Sometime during the early 1950's Mrs. Connie May had been visiting friends in Cambridge Road. It was very late when she left and there was no street lighting then but she had refused the husband's offer to see her home as she did not have far to go. However she did begin to feel uneasy because the tall hedges along the top of the high garden walls were so thick and dark. Connie tells the story:

'I was walking down Cambridge Road and suddenly this big black dog was walking beside me. I'm not keen on dogs but some how he was terribly comforting.' The dog walked all the way home with her, only stopping as they reached her gate and sitting down outside it when she went inside. Everybody had gone to bed so she went straight upstairs and peeped out of the bedroom window to look at him but he was gone. She never saw him again.

2: The Blue Hand of Etheldreda

St. Etheldreda, daughter of Anna, King of the East Angles, founded a convent for men and women at Ely in the 7th century. She used high land given as a wedding present by her first husband, Tondbert, Prince of the Fens.

It would be fitting then, if her spirit were to inhabit the area, watching over the city that she founded. Yet the only part of St. Etheldreda, ethereal and actual, to remain in the Isle, is her left hand. The ghostly hand is said to haunt the back staircase at the 14th century Prior's House, now a boys' boarding house and part of the King's School. The earthly hand resides not far away in a niche behind a glass screen above the font of St. Etheldreda's Roman Catholic Church in Egremont Street.

Three dozing boarders in the turret room of Prior's House claim to have witnessed the illuminated blue hand gliding up the stairway towards them. The actual 7th century hand was mauvish white in colour when seen by Mallyan Thompson during its arrival at the Catholic Church in 1953 just in time for its golden jubilee celebrations.

It has turned black now. Kept in a relinquary, perhaps since 1539 when the saint's shrine was destroyed by order of Henry VIII, the hand had been protected from the air. While King Henry's iconoclastic vandals were smashing up the elaborately carved shrine and hurling out the body, did a defiant believer detach this small part of Etheldreda's anatomy and stuff it inside his tunic? If so it must have been very precious to him. In those days of superstition and ignorance, amputated hands were believed to have supernatural powers and often used by thieves to protect themselves at night while they worked. The Pannett Museum in Whitby displays one of these black, shrivelled human hands. ' The Hand of Glory,' usually cut from an executed criminal, was preserved by means of a special recipe. The Whitby hand was found in the door lintel of a house in Castleton. This murderer's hand had been severed at the wrist as he hung from the gibbet and used as a burglar's talisman. How much more cherished then must have been the hand of a saint. Almost three hundred years later in 1810 Etheldreda's hand was discovered inside a reliquary hidden in the priest's hole of a Sussex farmhouse belonging to the

St. Etheldreda

The Prior's House showing the small window of the turret staircase.

Brick mosaic of St. Etheldreda, founder of Ely, on the wall of the main entrance to Tesco's Store, Angel Drove, Ely.

Duke of Norfolk, head of the Catholics in England.

Etheldreda had become Abbess of Ely in 673 soon after leaving her second husband, King Egfrith of Northumbria in order to take her vows. She died six years later of a tumour on her neck and was buried as she wished, in the common graveyard. On 17th October 695 when the body was exhumed for translation into the church, it was found to be incorrupt and the wound healed.

After this great miracle the new saint was to move three more times before her body was eventually thrown out on the order of Henry VIII in 1539. In 970 she was moved inside the refounded Saxon church and then in the middle of the 11th century yet again into the present Norman building. Finally in 1254 the shrine moved to a most prestigious setting further down the east end of the cathedral. Wherever it stood, pilgrims flocked to Ely to visit the holy remains. How did these simple believers react when bones venerated for 800 years were unceremoniously dumped at the wish of a king? They must have been angry and confused. Some brave soul managed to salvage a hand. Perhaps other parts were saved too but later lost.

The Duke of Norfolk gave the holy relic to his estate agent Mr. Harting who passed it on in 1867 to his granddaughter Sister Aquinas, a Dominican nun at Stone in Staffordshire. There it remained until 1953 when it was passed on again by Mary Pritchard, chauffeur to the Mother General at Stone. She gave it to her brother Father Guy Pritchard, parish priest of St. Ethelreda's, in Ely. And so the much travelled hand returned home more than three hundred years later just in time for the 50th anniversary celebrations of the church's foundation in 1903 and a poltergeist in the adjacent presbytery stopped banging doors and was at peace.

Looking towards The North Range from the east end of the Cathedral.

(see page 19)

The North Range from the High Street.

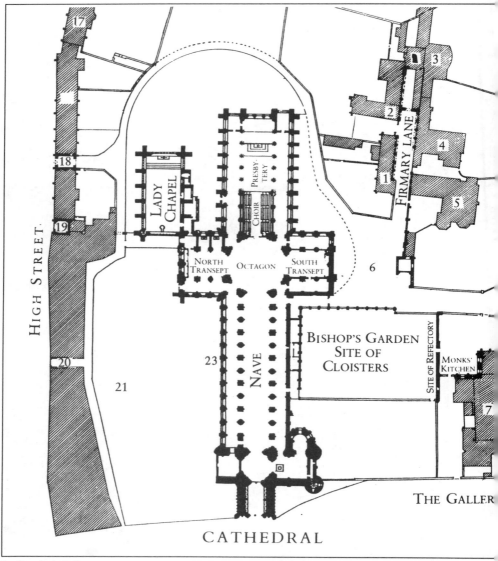

1. Powcher's Hall
2. Walsingham House (also known as The Painted Chamber and The Choir House.
3. The Chapter office / arrow showing... The Deanery
4. The Black Hostelry
5. Canonry House
6. Open area at top of Firmary Lane where Tony Ramsome saw a monk crossing and where Les Oakey and friends saw two arguing monks.
7. Bishop's House
8. The Prior's House
9. The Queens Hall
10. Prior Crauden's Chapel

The Monastic Buildings and the College at Ely

BY COURTESY OF ELY CATHEDRAL

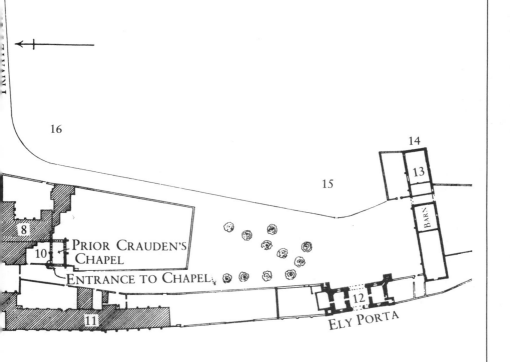

11. Monastic servants' quaters
12. The Porta
13. Monastic barn
14. Cherry Hill
15. The Park
16. The Dean's Meadow
17. (further along just off map) The Monk's Gate (Smiths the Cleaners)

18. (to the left) Ely Museum
19. The Goldsmith's Tower (Jumpers)
20. Steeple Gate
21. St. Cross Green
22. The Old Bishop's Palace
23. North Triforium

3: Monks

There were monks at Ely for over 800 years so it's natural that their presence should still be felt. Though the medieval buildings have been much altered and adapted to new uses over the centuries a great many of their former occupants manage to recognise and return to their old haunts.

THE NORTH RANGE

Some of the North Range monastic buildings remain backing onto the High Street but the Porta Monachorum or Monks' Gate has gone from the east end. Does the hooded Benedictine observed lurking round the back of Smiths the Cleaners by a previous manager imagine that the great gate still stands on this spot or has he merely got a dirty habit? Monks used to slip through this gate into the Market Square to visit their favourite inns and sample the strong local ale. The monastery ale 'was so weak that the pigs would not drink of it'.

And was it he who left two deep footprints in the snow of the museum yard just further down the street during the cold winter of 1991? The old fashioned sandal shaped prints were discovered by museum attendant Liz Nardone when she unlocked the back door soon after arriving. They faced the wall on the left side of the present door. Perhaps an earlier door once stood there when this part of the North Range was developed around 1325 by Sacrist, Alan of Walsingham. Nothing dripped down from above that might have caused the marks. The back gate remained locked; the rest of the yard was smooth and white. Liz has taken her camera to work every winter since but he hasn't been back. Could he have got cold feet and gone next door to 'Jumpers' where woollies fling themselves off the shelves during the night?

The North Range provided accommodation and work rooms for the skilled craftsmen who were working on the 14th century additions to the monastery, particularly the octagon and lantern. The goldsmith's workshop occupied the space now taken by 'Jumpers'.

Since the shop opened in 1989, manager Kate Marshall has been aware of a presence. She has arrived at work in the morning to find piles of knitwear swept off shelves onto the floor. This happens in the daytime too in front of other staff and

The goldsmith's workshop occupied the space now taken by 'Jumpers.'

The young monk stands by the counter below the camera.

customers. Kate has seen the probable culprit a few times in two separate places though he doesn't walk about. He's small, skinny and although his face is hidden inside the black hooded Benedictine robe, she knows he is very young. He stands either at the back of the shop in what used to be the yard or by the counter. Could he be mourning the loss of his tight knit community?

Yet further along the North Range is Steeple Gate where tourist trinkets throw themselves around in the downstairs gift shop and a presence is felt in the upstairs tea shop kitchen. A gateway has existed on this site since 1417 but the present plaster and timber building was erected in the 16th century to provide access to the churchyard and Cathedral.

The North Range, sandwiched between the monastery and the town was the area in which the lives of townspeople and monks overlapped but it was on the private south side of the abbey that the monks ate, slept and conducted their business. Here were the dormitory, refectory, kitchen, cloister, infirmary and chapter house. Not surprisingly this is the most haunted part of Ely.

FIRMARY LANE

On a bright moonlit autumn evening in 1984 school teacher Tony Ransome was hurrying along the path that leads round the east end of the Cathedral from the

North Range to Firmary Lane on the south side of the college when he glimpsed a shadowy figure in a long gown emerging from a small doorway in the south transept. The figure crossed in front of him and without replying to Tony's friendly greeting, he disappeared through the archway at the far side of the Lane. Both entrances have long been bricked up.

Les Oakey saw something peculiar in this same area in 1944 when he was a young lad during the war. He and two friends were approaching Firmary Lane from the opposite direction of the Porta Gate . It was very dark because of the black out. They were walking towards the south transept intending to go round the east end of the cathedral to the High Street. As they came to the open space by the bricked in cloister where Tony saw his monk in 1984, they found a little Jewish evacuee boy called Schwartz cowering against the wall. He was white, trembling all over and unable to speak but he grabbed hold of Les and pointed towards the south transept where the slype (a passage way) once ran between the original chapter house and the south transept. It was a place where the monks were allowed to talk and discuss, something they were not normally expected to do while carrying out their daily duties.

They all saw the figures of two monks arguing and shouting at each other. They took off back in the direction of the Porta. Young Schwartz was probably staying just round the corner at the Jews' Free School accommodated in old Hereward Hall in the Gallery during the war.

It was at the bottom of this atmospheric lane that writer Elizabeth Goudge lived with her parents during the early part of this century. In her autobiography 'The Joy of the Snow' Elizabeth describes the ghost she encountered in her home, the Deanery, a building now shared with the Chapter office, during her childhood in Ely.

Elizabeth was eleven when she and her parents moved to the city not long before the outbreak of the first world war. Her father had accepted a canonry at the cathedral combined with the principalship of the Theological College, now part of the Kings School. Elizabeth says that of all the places she ever lived 'for me Ely was the home of homes' in spite of the abundance of its ghosts, or possibly because of them.

'It is not striking outside, for the Victorian addition has made it sunny but not beautiful, but the heart of the house is Norman.'

The Deanery can be approached from the back way down Firmary Lane, once the Norman nave of the monks' infirmary but now open to the sky. The aisles where sick and senile monks once slept have been infilled with brick and converted into homes for present day clergy and King's School boarders. At the bottom of the lane the nave of the infirmary chapel, now an entrance yard, leads to the Chapter office formerly the Goudge family kitchen and in monastic times the bottom half of the chapel chancel. Divided by a floor, the Chapter office lies below and the present Dean's study above. The Rev. Henry Leighton Goudge had also used this upper room as his study.

Looking down Firmary Lane towards the Chapter Office yard and the back way to the Deanery.

The Front of the Deanery from Oyster Lane showing the Victorian additional storey above the first floor windows. (note the change in brickwork and open window of Elizabeth Goudge's former bedroom.)

'Here he prayed and worked on a level with the heads of the Norman arches, their capitals carved with the arrow headed reeds that grow in the fens.'

Strangely though, Elizabeth's monk did not appear in the medieval part of the house but in the 19th century second storey addition where she slept in the attic room facing Oyster Lane and Ely Park. She would wake up suddenly during the night and see him standing beside her bed.

'I would feel fear and revulsion, a sense of struggle as though I fought against something, and then he was gone.'

When Elizabeth asked if she might change her haunted bedroom for another her father decided to swap beds with her for one night so he could meet this 'phenomenon' before making his decision. But although he was kept awake all night by the scuttling of mice and the howling of the wind round the high attic window he saw nothing.

'He was not a man to see things, hear things or imagine things.'

However he agreed that she might change her room for a quieter one. So Elizabeth moved but the ghost followed. When she moved again he followed again.

'He was not a frequent visitor. Nor is he now. For I was not alone in seeing that ghost. Subsequent dwellers in the house have seen him too. I do not know how he appeared to them but to me he appeared as a grey-cowled monk with no face. Where his face should have been there was only darkness.'

In the summer of 1990 another cathedral family moved into the house where the Goudge family had lived eighty years earlier. Rev. Stephen Shipley the new Precentor was staying there with his wife Rosie and their young children while awaiting permanent accommodation. The attic bedroom was now part of a second floor flat but on the night when Rosie Shipley experienced the wandering ghost she was staying in a little room on the first floor. Her previous night's sleep had been disturbed by her son; her following night's sleep was to be disturbed by something worse.

In the *Ely Cathedral News* of April 1992 Rosie Shipley wrote about her experience.

'It was during the second or third night on my own that I was suddenly awoken by the sound of approaching footsteps......suddenly I was gripped with fear and, I'm ashamed to say I burrowed under the bedclothes. I lay there, frozen to the spot, heart pounding, unable to call out until the sensation subsided and I dared emerge.'

She put on the light and read for a while to calm herself down and then went back to sleep. Later on the whole episode happened again.

'I was awoken by the distinct sound of footsteps......I could hear the vibration of items on the piano with each step. Then once again I was seized with terror, again I dived under the bedclothes and again I experienced those nightmarish sensations.' As before the horror passed and she switched on the light and read a little. In the cold light of day the experiences of the night still seemed vivid and real.

'Imagine, then, the impact that a passage in Elizabeth Goudge's autobiography had on me when I happened to come across it less than a week later.............. While the external details were different - I had only heard footsteps while she saw a figure - I felt that Elizabeth Goudge could not have described my own experience better.'

The Shipleys soon moved from the Deanery flat and saw no more monks but Elizabeth had lived there for three years until she left for boarding school. As her mother was an invalid and her father often away from home she was obliged to walk alone down Firmary Lane to attend Evensong in the Cathedral.

'...if I went out of the back door and down the lane there was a haunted house on my right and another on my left and either ghost might issue out; not to mention our own ghost who had probably walked out of the house behind me and at any moment might lay his hand on my shoulder as we went along.'

The haunted house on Elizabeth's right was The Painted Chamber. It is now the boarding house for King's School choir boys but was once a hall built for Alan of Walsingham . Thoughtfully he allowed the female relations of sick or senile monks to stay there while visiting.

According to Elizabeth ' The family who lived there had seen nothing but had been weighed down with a sense of misery in a certain part of the house.'

When alterations to the house required the removal of an old wall the skeleton of a monk was found behind it. The bones were buried and the building exorcised but Elizabeth...'could seldom walk down the lane without horrible thoughts of what

The entrance to Walsingham House where the skeleton of a walled up monk was found.

it must feel like to be walled up.'

What terrible crime could the unhappy monk have committed to be given such a cruel punishment? Sir Walter Scott's poem, *Marmian* tells of a nun, Constance de Beverley, of Whitby Abbey who falls in love with a bold but fickle knight and is walled up as punishment for breaking her vows. Could something similar have happened at Ely?

Perhaps a monk attending the adjacent infirmary for his monthly blood letting session caught a glimpse of one of the visiting female relations and was tempted to sin? If so the sin must have taken place before the blood letting. Documentary evidence from the Middle Ages suggests that this practice- was widely followed by monks in order to subdue their 'sensual desires'. It is thought that enough blood was taken for the monk to lose consciousness, probably about three pints a month. At one of Britain's most important medieval hospitals, Soutra, near Edinburgh, blood dumps found preserved in the local clay seem to confirm this practice.

A house mistress who lived at Walsingham House in the 1970's heard her baby and toddler screaming one evening not long after she had put them to bed. She ran up the stairs three at a time to find them both quite hysterical for no apparent reason. This kind of thing seems to be a common occurrence in old houses. *Midland Ghosts and Hauntings* has an almost identical story told by a mother living in a 16th century cottage in the medieval part of Alvechurch.

The Black Hostelry where a male guest 'was reputed to have rushed headlong from the house in terror.'

'The boys slept in the front bedroom and every night they woke up screaming. They had never woken in the night, so I moved them into a back bedroom where they slept peacefully.'

The house on Elizabeth's left which she says 'had something rather nasty' was the Black Hostelry, so called because visiting Benedictine monks in their black robes stayed here. Elizabeth tells us that a male guest 'was reputed to have rushed headlong from the house in terror.' Others too have sensed an unwelcoming atmosphere in the area. This must surely have been cancelled out by the welcoming atmosphere radiated by the ecclesiastical couple who now run the Black Hostelry as a 20th century bed and breakfast hostelry.

Strangely Elizabeth seems to have missed the monk who peers out through the back window of Powcher's Hall, the building next to Walsingham along Firmary Lane. The bottom walls of the front of this house were constructed by infilling the Norman arches of the infirmary aisle with bricks sometime after the monastery was dissolved in the 16th century but the upper floor was reputedly the monks' blood-letting hall. The monks surely enjoyed their health visits to Powcher's Hall because, as well as the odd glimpse of a female visitor, their duties were relaxed and their diet improved. A record of the menu for the week beginning 1st August 1388 includes 'beef, mutton, pork, veal, pullets, capons, salt and fresh fish, eggs, milk, cream, mustard, cheese, and spices.'

In 1947 eleven year old Margaret E. came to live at Powcher's Hall with her mother who had become housekeeper to bachelor Canon

Powcher's Hall (on the left) home of Canon Ratcliff between 1947 and 1958.

Ratcliff, Professor of Divinity at Ely. Not long after they arrived she was sitting in a window seat on the top floor with her new friend Rani, the siamese cat when they heard footsteps coming up the stairs. They both turned towards the sound but when nobody appeared Margaret called out. She wanted her mother to see how intelligently Rani was behaving. There was no answer so she went to investigate and found her mother downstairs baking in the kitchen. The Professor was out.

Once when Mrs. E. was in the garden hanging out washing she noticed a monk looking out of the small window next to the back door. Assuming the Professor had a visitor, she rushed inside to put the kettle on. Clerical looking gentlemen were often calling to visit and she always made tea for them. She took the loaded tray into the study but Canon Ratcliff was alone and rather surprised to see the tea tray set for two. However the Canon was always interested to hear about odd happenings in the house as he too had heard things. All three of them used to listen to quick light footsteps tripping along the upstairs corridor. They moved in the direction of the big drawing room with the window overlooking the cathedral and were followed by the sound of the door opening and shutting. Yet Margaret insists that none of them were susceptible or nervous.

Margaret once saw a monk in her bedroom wearing a white habit. He talked to her and though she tried hard she could not understand his language. She described

Powcher's Hall

him later to the professor who recognised him as being from a certain order not usually seen at Ely which was a Benedictine monastery. It was a long time ago and she can't remember the name of the order.

While the professor was away on business Margaret's grandma came to visit. During the night there was a lot of noise on the top floor but the three females were too afraid to investigate. Grandma suggested that they all stay under the covers and let the supposed burglars take what they wanted. In the morning they went upstairs together expecting to find a mess but everything was just as it should have been. In 1958 Canon Ratcliff moved to Cambridge to become the Regius Professor of Divinity. Mrs. E. and Margaret went with him. They were all sad to leave their ghosts behind as they had become part of the family.

THE CATHEDRAL
Two contented monks haunt Ely Cathedral. The first one regularly attends Evensong. Derek Butler, late Head Verger, used to tell of a member of the congregation who was sitting in the choir during Evensong talking to himself. On his way out he asked Derek if he knew who was the friendly clerical gentleman sitting beside him during the service. Derek remarked that he had noticed he was sitting alone but the man insisted he had been talking to a nice old man in a long black robe.

He's gone now', he told Derek 'but when we stopped to speak he was behind you.' Derek didn't see him at all.

Stained Glass Museum invigilator Jill Peak glimpsed 'Brother Thomas' in the

Powcher's Hall from the garden side facing the Cathedral.

autumn of 1993 in the north triforium, where the museum was then located.

'It seems funny that for such an important event I never made any record of it in my diary. I suppose at the time it was so incredible I thought I should always remember.'

The north triforium is a long, narrow area with a single doorway at the east end. Jill had paused half way down to pick up a dropped ticket when movement near the door caught her eye. It was a person moving from left to right.

'At first I thought it was a woman in a long black coat and Paddington Bear hat. It was an extremely solid figure that I saw. I thought she had gone into the alcove to look at the medieval glass.'

Jill got up and moved towards the alcove intending to ask the woman to pay but there was no one there. The door was always in view so it was impossible for anyone to have left. At this point there was a dramatic drop in temperature. It became bitterly cold. Jill had never felt such intense cold. Even the temperature at the Christmas Eve carol service had never dropped as low as this. Her curiosity was roused and suddenly she knew that the woman in black was a Benedictine monk. The Paddington Bear hat was a cowl. The name 'Brother Thomas' popped into her head.

'What I'd seen was a monk. I didn't feel afraid.... although my hair stood on end. Quite quickly afterwards the temperature went back to normal and I had this incredible feeling of serenity and peace and that hung around for a long time

The Stained Glass Museum when it was housed in the North Triforium showing the only exit.

afterwards till I went home. I came to the conclusion that yes, I'd seen my second ghost.'

(Jill's first ghost was not a monk. He was Canon Bawtree and she can put a date to this sighting. He died about November 1988 and she saw him in February 1989 at 6pm walking through the park with his Collie dog in the old familiar way with his hands behind his back holding the lead. When she looked again they had vanished.)

The rest of the museum staff have never seen Jill's 'Brother Thomas'. Jill hasn't seen him since but sometimes while sitting behind her desk in the Stained Glass Museum she feels peace and serenity, love and warmth.

'I feel that 'Brother Thomas' and I have something in common. We both love this place and maybe that's why he comes and says hello.'

THE BISHOP'S PALACE

The final monk likes to make himself useful and he has certainly come back to the right place. The 15th century old Bishop's Palace has been used as various kinds of hospital since 1938 and was taken over by the Sue Ryder organisation in 1986. The staff in this nursing home for the sick and disabled welcome voluntary help but they do prefer to direct the volunteers. One day during the early 1990's an old man in a wheelchair went missing for a couple of hours and was eventually discovered still strapped into his chair sitting peacefully in the chapel. He was able to propel himself but couldn't walk and as the chapel was down three steep steps nobody bothered to look for him in there for a long time. When he was eventually found and asked how he had managed to get to the chapel he replied that a kind monk had negotiated his wheelchair down the steps.

4: The Angel in the Moonlight

Elizabeth Goudge said of her faceless ghost: 'He was not a pleasant person, not like the angel figure who haunted the next door house but one.'

The next door house but one is Canonry House, now a girls' boarding house for the King's School. Built in the 12th century as the Cellarer's Hall its 14th, 18th and 19th century additions have turned it into a spacious hotch potch. The original rectangular stone building has been almost enclosed. It can hardly be recognised as medieval from the outside though its Firmary Lane side wall is constructed of infilled Norman archways behind which 20th century additions of showers and changing rooms have been added. They will amaze the Cellarer if he ever comes back for a look round. He probably bathed three times a year at the most. He was a powerful obedientiary and would have been responsible for all the monastery provisions including the wines and ales which would be kept in the cool undercroft. He would have had tenements and estates to provide food stuffs for his office.

Elizabeth tells us:

'The apparition was so unusual that Canon and Mrs. Glazebrook, who lived in the house at that time, came to the conclusion that it was not a ghost at all. For what ghost stands still to have its portrait painted?'

Mrs. Glazebrook was an amateur painter but instead of selecting a bowl of roses or the lantern tower of Ely Cathedral to copy, she chose the unusual subject of the resident ghost. It was surely an inspired choice. It is unlikely that the sitter would get a sudden urge to scratch its nose or turn its head to look out of the window. It probably wouldn't ask to be made thinner or have its warts removed. But what could have been Canon Glazebrook's opinion of the subject of his wife's painting? He was probably just glad she had a little hobby to keep her busy. Elizabeth saw the portrait when the proud artist showed it to her mother. While Mrs. Goudge was perhaps thinking of positive remarks to make like 'It's better than I could do' or 'I like the colours,' her daughter was taking a good look and observed later to her diary that the painting was of 'a figure in a long robe, resembling a saint in a stained-glass window.'

Yet although the painting showed an unusually attractive ghost some of the Glazebrook's visitors were afraid of it 'for it appeared in the spare room, and guests

Canonry House

from the outside world were not acclimatised to the unexplainable as we were who lived always in the shadow of history and legend.'

One unsuspecting guest soon regretted her decision to have an early night when she saw 'the beautiful figure who stood in the moonlight against a blank wall.' She was too terrified to move but luckily there was a bell rope by the bed so she was able to call the servant while still cowering under the covers. The old servant wasn't very sympathetic as she regarded the angel as a member of the household.

'I can see it in my room too and I call it my angel. When the moonlight leaves the wall it will go.'

The odd thing about this ghost was that it only appeared when bright moonlight shone on a certain part of the wall both in the guest room and above in the old maid's room.

'It was so to speak a double ghost, slightly smaller in the upper room.'

It could have been the reflection of a stained glass window cast on the wall by the moonlight only there wasn't any such window.

'Another theory advanced by someone was that the bright moonlight brought out the outline of some hidden fresco.'

But this wouldn't happen in two rooms.

Although the present girl boarders have not seen the Angel in the Moonlight some of them did notice a little girl in a nightie with bare feet who recently attended their fire drill. She didn't join them on the corridor but stood alone in the Norman archway opposite.

5: Silver Street Cottages

The cottages at numbers 7, 9 and 11 Silver Street were originally one building, a late medieval hall house, though there had been some kind of house on the site since at least 1310. Number 7 would have been the parlour with upstairs solar, number 9, the hall with open hearth and number 11, the buttery and pantry with upstairs chamber. The house was probably divided sometime during the 19th century but the ghosts who visit take little notice of such recent alterations.

Jo and Andrew Odell - Rourke and their new baby moved into number 11 in April 1993. Jo used to think she could hear him crying in the upstairs room and would rush up the stairs only to find him fast asleep. This happened a few times.

Sometimes she sees a fair haired young man wearing a white shirt with a large collar and ruffled front and cuffs. She calls him Adrian. When he is downstairs he walks through the east wall into number 9 and although this middle occupant has never seen him, she often smells lavender and sometimes wood smoke.

The crown-post roof of this centre cottage was encrusted with soot, evidence that an open fire once burned in the middle of the room and perhaps accounting for the smell of wood smoke. Early paintings discovered on the west end wall of this room in 1987 are thought to be 14th century. Naturalistic vine scroll patterns cover the plaster work between the wooden beams. The paintings probably decorated the wall behind the raised dais on which the owner and his family would have sat when dining. Perhaps lavender would be strewn upon the earth floor to mask the cooking smells. The adjoining wall and fireplace would not have existed when the cottages were a Hall house.

Jo has seen the young man in her bedroom too, in the middle of the night. He leans on the corner of the chest of drawers deep in thought. She says 'Go away Adrian and let me sleep' and he disappears. More recently Jo and the children have heard the sound of a latch being raised as though the living room door were opening. They look up and say 'Here's daddy coming' but it is only 'Adrian.' He walks through the wall into the garden.

In the late 1980s an Australian couple were visiting the previous tenant of Number 7 and stayed in the room that would have been the first floor solar of the

Hall House. Rare and delicate 15th century wall paintings of birds were discovered in this room and restored in 1987. During the night while the man was sleeping, his wife woke and sat up in bed so she could get a closer look at a medieval lady sitting in the corner of the room examining her jewels. She wore a long, pale gown with a white kerchief over her hair. Glinting jewels were held before her in both hands. Such magical paintings could not fail to attract visitors from the past but the present occupant of the cottage has never seen, felt or smelt any thing unusual.

Yet while the cottage was being restored in 1987 even the painters felt a presence and their brushes had been moved about whenever they returned from their tea break.

Adrian's door in part of the medieval hall house now no. 7 Silver Street.

6: Oliver Cromwell

Ely's ghost population wouldn't be complete without that of its most famous citizen Oliver Cromwell and it is probably his ghost that haunts Oliver Cromwell House, now the Tourist office but for many years the vicarage of St. Mary's Parish Church.

Cromwell came to Ely when he inherited land and buildings through his mother Elizabeth Steward whose family had farmed at Ely for several generations. Both she and her brother Thomas were born in the manor house that stood on Stuntney Hill by the Newmarket road. Sadly it fell down during the 1950s after lying derelict for many years. Now only an ancient barn remains.

Could it be Elizabeth or her mother, Katherine who strolls across the A142 on murky nights towards dusk causing nervous motorists to swerve and blow their horns? Certainly it is a woman for she wears a long grey gown and carries a basket as she picks her way carefully along the path that used to lead from the manor house to Stuntney village now on the opposite side of the main road. At this place where the old and new roads cross horses shy and side step when trotting up Stuntney Hill. Elizabeth married Robert Cromwell of Hinchinbrook House in Huntingdon where their son Oliver was born in 1599.

Oliver didn't come to live in Ely until 1636 when he, the single surviving male descendent among seven sisters, inherited his childless uncle's houses and estates as well as the post 'farmer of the tithes.' He moved with his wife, his mother, two unmarried sisters and six children into the rectory, now Ely Tourist office since 1990. It is the only existing house, other than Hampton Court Palace, where Cromwell is know to have lived for any length of time. The building '...consisted of a fair Parsonage house built with brick and stone, and covered with tyles, containing a hall, a parlour, a kitchen, buttery, larder, milkhouse and other -necessary Rooms with Chambers over them. A fair Parsonage Barn called ye Sextry Barn standing within the yard, with other necessary out houses and lodges pertaining to the barn called ye Grange.'

It was from this house where the Cromwells lived between 1636 and 1647, that Oliver, as a man of wealth and property, was able to rise to become the most

Only a single barn remains standing to remind us of Stuntney Old Hall,
once home of Oliver Cromwell's mother and grandmother.

powerful man in England after the execution of Charles 1 in 1649. Part of the house dates back to the 13th century but it is in the early 17th century addition that a charismatic male presence has been felt. This west wing built in 1615 consisted of the Tithe Office on the ground floor with a room above. From the window of this room Cromwell might have looked down to watch laden carts bringing local produce into the yard for storage in the great barn that stood adjacent to the courtyard.

This room became the guest bedroom during the time that Canon Neil Munt and his wife Joan lived in the vicarage from 1974 to 1986 and it was in here that their friends Brian and Marion stayed when they came to visit in April 1979. Marion tells the story.

'I had slept for a while and then woken as usual. While I was awake, Brian got up and went to the toilet. He returned a minute or so later and went back to sleep.'

But Marion remained awake and without remembering how she got there, suddenly found herself standing in a corner of the room. The door should have been to the right but instead there was a small dark doorway in front of her. Her bare feet could feel rough floorboards yet she knew that the room was carpeted.

'My arms were being gripped tightly by a man's hands. I was holding my arms, bent at the elbow, in front of me so that my hands were in front of his chest. My fingers could feel under them a rough suede leather coat or jerkin. I could not see anyone but I had a clear impression of a powerful and determined personality who was also physically powerful.'

Stuntney Old Hall drawn by Henry Baines about 1860.

Yet Marion knew she was in no danger. On the contrary she felt a deep bond with her captor. Although he did not speak to her, she knew that he had recently made a decision that would change the course of both their lives; but was that her own life or that of a person in another time? She felt afraid for him and of the changes this decision would make.

'In my mind, but not I think spoken aloud, was the phrase "Tis not my way" said again and again. Yet I accepted that the decision had been made. Although his grip on my arms was tight I had no thought that he intended to hurt me - it was expression of his determination to pursue his course of action.'

At the time Marion understood the decision and knew her captor's name yet could not remember either three days later when she was typing out the account of her experiences. She knew she had wanted to wake her husband but couldn't. She felt that she was part of two separate existences yet could not reach either.

Suddenly the man released his hold and the door faded. Feeling very cold and tired, Marion went back to bed and slept till morning. When she finally woke her arms were aching. She pushed back the covers to discover red finger marks around both arms, but showing stronger on the left. She showed Brian but didn't say anything as she needed time to think. When she finally told him what had happened he went upstairs to examine the room and found the old lintel post and frame where the original doorway had been plastered over. The new doorway and gallery corridor were an extension of 1763 built onto the rear of the original 14th-15th century part of the house.

The window of the haunted bedroom with the Tithe Office doorway below at Oliver Cromwell house.

The lintel post and frame of the blocked up doorway in the haunted bedroom.

What was it that so troubled this man that he cannot lie quiet in his graves? What was the decision he took that was not his way? The execution of Charles, an anointed king and the Fenland legend of the Grey Goose Feather both spring to mind.

The legend tells of a time during the civil war when King Charles was fleeing northward through the Fens from Oxford. He is said to have spent the night at Snowre Hall, Fordham, near Downham Market with Royalist sympathisers but was stopped by Cromwell's Fen soldiers as he left the house. Charles showed them a split grey goose feather and they let him go. When Cromwell found out he did not punish them.

'They were Fenmen and so they had to help anyone who was carrying a split goose feather.'

He knew it was better for a king to escape than for a Fenman to break his vow.

Then on the eve of the execution as Cromwell was about to dine, a messenger from Charles brought him a split grey goose feather and said; 'Sir, His Majesty is too proud to ask for mercy but he does ask to be given the help that's given to anyone who shows this.'

Cromwell sent away the food and the next morning the servant found him 'still sitting at the table and staring at the quill.'

Was it Cromwell that Marion encountered in the west bedroom at Ely Rectory in April 1979 and could this have been the decision that caused him such unease? His signature on the 1649 death warrant was only one of 57 yet it was possibly the most important.

Over lunch Brian explained what had happened to the Munts, their daughter Alison and her friend. They all examined the marks which by now were beginning to fade. Alison knew the room was haunted. Although she had seen nothing herself, she had once heard a man's footsteps in the adjoining corridor followed by the sound of a door opening and shutting. Alison and Marion then discovered that several years previously but on separate occasions they had each seen a woman in a long dark blue skirt going up the stairs. Neither had mentioned it before.

This could have been the same woman seen by Kate and Angela Marshall when they were staying at the vicarage with Revd Jack Bagley and Mrs. Bagley, friends of their parents. Jack Bagley was vicar of Ely from 1963 to 1974 and the girls had stayed with his family on several occasions.

'My sister and I stayed with the Bagleys for a few days during the summer holidays. We were giggling and chatting in the night and had we been at home we would have been shouted at by father but we fell silent when a lady wearing a long dark dress with keys at the waist came into the room. She had dark hair, no hat, and just looked at us, turned and went out.'

Kate saw this ghost again a few years later while staying at the house to look after the Bagley's grandson while his parents were in Hong Kong. The Bagleys didn't find it unusual. They had seen her frequently.

CROMWELL'S FEN SOLDIERS

Because of Cromwell's position in the local community he was able to reinforce his strict and uncompromising puritan ideas with appropriate action and so he made enemies. In January 1643 he marched into the cathedral with his soldiers during the choir service without even taking off his hat and told everyone to leave. Cromwell did not approve of singing in church. He thought it 'unedifying and offensive'. He locked the door and put the key in his pocket. The cathedral possibly remained closed for seventeen years.

In 'God's Englishman,' Christopher Hill says of Cromwell:

'we see him in the early months of the war rounding up all pockets of royalist resistance in his area, seizing arms, raising and training troupe, calling for money.' The following tale from Bunty Jones of her experiences while baby-sitting at The Chantry on Palace Green in the early 1970's seems to reflect this view.

The eighteenth century Chantry House is just across the grass from Cromwell House but the scene described by Bunty must refer to the earlier building that stood on this site. The original 12th century Chantry Chapel was further east.

Bunty was baby-sitting for the Bristols who still live in Chantry House though their children are grown up now. About midnight, while she was watching television, the room suddenly turned cold. Bunty heard the sound of heavy boots marching about and doors banging. Male voices were shouting quite close by, perhaps in the next room. She was unable to move from her chair.

After about fifteen minutes the noise faded, the room became warmer and she was able to get up. She ran upstairs to look at the children but they were asleep. As soon as the Bristols returned she went home not waiting for an explanation. Much later she described her nasty experience to Mrs. Bristol who was not surprised. Her husband had heard the soldiers though she never had. The previous owners of Chantry House had told the Bristols that Cromwell's Roundheads came to take away the men who lived there. At the beginning of the civil war some of Cromwell's local soldiers wore their hair very short and so earned the name 'Roundheads.' These soldiers were hand picked by Cromwell from around the Fens for their strength, loyalty and stoicism but another characteristic of Fen people is that they do tend to have very round heads.

Bunty never went back to Chantry House.

The Chantry on Palace Green.

7: Nell Gwynne

It wasn't just the appearance and character of the High Street that was diminished when the graceful bay window above Peck's ironmonger's shop was removed in the 1920's and replaced with a flat frame and plain glass. Part of Ely's past breathed in the fabric of the materials. Nell Gwynne, saucy mistress of King Charles II in the late 17th century, was reputed to recline in that window seat and gaze longingly down the High Street in the direction of the Bishop's Palace. According to Jean Eames, the great-grand daughter of George Peck who founded the firm in the 19th century, Charles and Nell had come over to Ely from Newmarket races to look at a horse. Local tales suggest that the horse was the legendary Highflyer, bred in Bury St. Edmunds and sold to Richard Tattersall of Highflyer Farm near Ely in 1779 for £2500 after winning eight races and 800 guineas in a sweepstake. However as Charles and Nellie visited Ely about a hundred years before Highflyer was born they must have been inspecting some other horse.

Naturally Bishop Gunning as Ely's first citizen would have offered King Charles the finest accommodation in the city, his own home, The Bishop's Palace on the Green. It might have been around this time that he planted the plane tree in his garden that continues to flourish over three hundred years later. Perhaps King Charles walked in the gardens by the young plane tree, probably the oldest and largest in England. In any case Nell did not walk in the gardens. The Bishop frowned on the alliance the King had made with a common orange seller and didn't think it proper that she should stay on religious property. Bishop Gunning would have had some authority with Charles. He didn't take kindly to Parliament's interference in his life but would almost certainly have listened to a Bishop, especially one who had been imprisoned as a Royalist during the Civil War. In those days Bishops played an important role as advisers to kings. So 'Pretty, witty Nell' as Samuel Peyps called her in his diary, was obliged to lodge across the High Street in the secular part of the City. The property with the elegant first floor bay window was then a private house but later became E. Wilton's, Boot and Shoe shop and then during the 19th century, Pecks ironmongers. After the house and shop were mutilated in 1910 Nell's ghost had to abandon her window seat view but according to some of

Drawing of Peck's ironmonger's shop showing Nell Gwynne's bay window drawn by Henry Baines about 1860.

the present staff odd things still happen in the cellars and on the first floor.

Another tale suggests that Nell Gwynne stayed at the north end of Broad Street in one of a fine range of timbered Tudor houses that were demolished in the 1930's to make way for a timber merchant's showroom. The house on the left of the range was known as 'Nell Gwynne's House.' In January 1994 an Ely fireman who was living in a flat further along Broad Street on the opposite side from the site of the timbered row heard a woman's voice calling 'Help! Help!' He thought the voice came from the area of St. Peter's church so he ran across the road and looked down both sides but couldn't find anything. St. Peter's was built in 1889 'to accommodate the needs of the increased population of the area' so there were plenty of people around who might have needed help. When the fireman told his colleagues about his experience they laughed and said he must have been drinking. Then one evening in March he heard the voice again pleading with him to help. He said out loud 'I'll help you. I'll do what I can.' The voice stopped and he didn't hear it again.

It is unlikely that Nell Gwynne would have been in trouble. She was under the protection of a King and presumably safe from harm. But Broad Street was Ely's first thoroughfare and principal trading and industrial area from the middle ages as it was so near the river highway. It has long been a highly populated area of the city and a surfeit of public houses catered for the busy water trade. Lots of narrow lanes led down to the quayside. The Ship Inn was at the bottom of one and the Cutter Inn at the bottom of another. The Black Swan stood opposite the St. Peter's end of Broad Street with the Angel further along. This combination of pubs and watermen would almost certainly produce situations where somebody needed help.

8: The Sergeant-Major, the Irish Woman and the Nurse

The Cambridgeshire Militia was revived around the time of the Crimean war although there had been a 'Loyal Association of Volunteers' at Ely since the end af the 18th century. These were a reserve force who could be called on to assist the regular army when needed. Scottish Sergeant-Major John Kyle must have been part of this early force as he enlisted in 1793, served with the Duke of Wellington in Belgium in 1794 and later in Flanders, Holland, Hanover and the West Indies before finally becoming Sergeant-Major of the Cambridgeshire Militia in 1802. Although he was discharged with a pension in 1852 he continued to live in Ely and was a familiar sight around town with his old friends Sergeant Cuttris and Quartermaster Sergeant Knott.

Sergeant-Major Kyle lived long enough to learn about the start of the new war and to watch a rusty Russian cannon arrive at Ely Station on June 26th 1860 and be pulled up the hill to Palace Green by a team of six horses. It had been captured at the Battle of Sebastapol and 'graciously bestowed on the city of Ely' by Queen Victoria She was invited to Ely to inspect the newly formed volunteers but declined and sent the cannon instead accompanied by the band of the Grenadier Guards. The old soldier died six months later in December aged 87. He was buried in the cemetery with his old red jacket as a shroud and a thistle carved on his tombstone. A tribute to his memory in the Cambridge Chronicle, June 13th 1863 observed:

'The deceased was often cheered during his service by the commendations of his superior officers for his zeal and ability and eventually retired with full pay of his rank, which he enjoyed for some time, when he died in a good old age, respected by military men who could appreciate the noble bearing of an old soldier.'

Could he be the Sergeant-Major who marches down Silver Street on late Spring afternoons wearing a smart red jacket? The upright old soldier stays on the left side of the street and turns the corner into Parade Lane. The militia Sergeant-Majors usually lived in the end house on Parade Lane nearest to Silver Street, so he could

The Canon on the Green captured from the Russians at the Battle of Sebastapol.

be going home for his tea.

All the permanent Militia staff lived in the Silver Street area The Adjutant's house stood on the site of the present Walpole Court. The stores and armoury were next door. The quartermaster probably lived in one of the four militia houses opposite the Prince Albert public house and some of the sergeants lived in Parade Lane, previously called Smock Mill Alley. The Parade Ground occupied the site of the present car park. The volunteers, who were mainly agricultural labourers from the surrounding area, were billeted with local families. They would come to Ely for three weeks usually in May and train as soldiers under officers taken from the local gentry. As soon as their uniforms were donned those awkward fen farm labourers were transformed. There was no difficulty finding billets in the local community for the dashing red coats. They livened up the limited local social life and were consequently very popular. However as the late Lt Col Archer observed 'human souvenirs' tended to appear nine months later. And as Charles Dickens wrote in 1837 (Pickwick Papers) 'A good uniform must work its way with the women, sooner or later.'

In 1869 permanent headquarters were added to house the sergeants and a hospital 'sufficiently large to accommodate thirty invalid soldiers.' This area, then known as the Barracks but now renamed The Range, contained 'twelve substantial neat looking residences, each one containing five rooms, an outhouse and water closet separated by divisions.'

In the late 1970's Annie (not her real name) moved to one of these 'neat looking residences.' She had only been there for a few weeks when one morning in summertime she woke early just as it was getting light to see a woman standing by the side of the bed looking at her. Annie describes her as a handsome, healthy woman probably in her late thirties with plentiful black hair and wearing a dazzlingly white apron. Annie knew instinctively that she was Irish. She looked Irish. She was 'quite solid but the soldier who stood behind her was small and shadowy.' Annie was not afraid but remembers being very surprised at the whiteness of the apron. How did she get it so clean? Annie had an impression of three or four children just inside the door peeping round their parents. She knew they were ghosts as it was early morning and the doors were locked. There was an atmosphere but not coldness. She spoke to the young woman; 'Did you once live here?'

The family remained a moment and then were gone. Annie never saw them again though she lived in that house for ten years.

Four years later she told this story to Christine Pownell who had moved next door in 1981. Christine was interested in the history of The Range and was doing research at Cambridge Library. In the census of 1881 she discovered that Seargent Atkins and his wife Emma had lived in that house and that Emma was from County Limerick. They had eight children at that time (if she was about 35) but later had triplet boys and received 'the usual bounty' of £3. Sadly the Atkins family lost a little daughter, Mary Maud aged about 2, who accidentally drowned in a tub in the back

The Militia Hospital and twelve substantial residences for sergeants.

Photo of the Militia Hospital and Barracks now renamed The Range. Photograph by Tom Bolton, early 19th century Ely photographer.

yard. It's a three bedroom house and the very small wash house was outside. With such a large family to wash for, perhaps Emma put her wash tub in the back yard during good weather. No wonder Annie marvelled at the dazzling whiteness of the apron!

The old lady next door saw a man in uniform sitting in her garden. He was dressed in khaki with red trimmings.

Although the Cambridgeshire Militia only continued in Ely until 1908 the hospital was possibly used again between 1915 and 1919 for casualties of the first world war. The Nurse who walks down the lane from the hospital holding a lamp to guide her footsteps wears a long dark dress and a small light kerchief over her hair. She looks Victorian and seems more likely to have come back from the Militia period of the hospital's history. The nurse crosses Silver Street without waiting for traffic. She is obviously not familiar with the motor car.

9: Waterside Antiques

Brewing was one of the most important of Ely's local industries from the 13th century continuing until the mid 20th and as the industry needed water and good communications, all of Ely's many breweries were near the river. William Marsh owned the Waterside brewery during the 17th century but by the late 18th century it belonged to brothers A. and B. Hall. After they moved the business to Forehill, the maltings was used as a storage barn. The Hall brothers lived in two houses round the back where there were also stables, a blacksmith's shop and work shops where barrels were made and pub signs painted.

Graham Peters leased the L-shaped former maltings from Barbara and Tim Eaton in March 1986 and started converting it for use as an antique shop complex. A single workman sandblasting downstairs in the foot of the L-shaped building that lies away from the road heard footsteps above in the area that Graham used as a workshop and where he kept his expensive tools. The workman ascended the only staircase to investigate. The workshop was at the back of the first floor but on a lower level down a steep ramp. It was empty and the floor covered with undisturbed dust. The Eaton's bulldog, Oscar had always refused to go beyond that ramp. Later Graham noticed that other dogs refused to go beyond it too. One of the workmen owned a highly obedient Labrador but even this dog disobeyed orders in that part of the barn. He insisted on edging round the wall to get past that spot. Elizabeth Goudge had noticed the extra sense possessed by dogs. She wrote:

'My dogs have always known far more than I do; but then the power of animals are so exquisite that ours dwindle to nothing beside them.'

When the maltings had been in use the oast house occupied the foot of the L-shape but it was removed in 1972 because the wooden tower was rotten. All the beams were replaced but the roof was not relined, so it is always colder in this part of the building. It seems an odd spot for a ghost as there wouldn't have been a floor there originally. Presumably the atmosphere so disliked by dogs is rising from the ground floor. The downstairs area was set out as an emergency morgue during the second war but was probably never used. Ely's R.A.F. hospital in Lynn Road, built before the war as a special burns unit had its own facilities. Wounded airmen of all

Graham tries out his divining rods.

nationalities were brought there for treatment. Graham's mother in law, Joan Griffin, used to visit them in hospital when she was a young girl living up Lynn Road. Her mother took in relatives of the burned airmen when they came to visit. There were lots of deaths and according to Joan their bodies were laid out in the Waterside maltings until being collected by relatives or sent to the cemetery near Marshall's airport in Cambridge. Others who lived in Waterside during the war believe that the facility was never used.

Yet since the antique complex opened in November 1986 at least a dozen separate customers have remarked on the oppressive nature of that particular area. As Graham has not advertised his ghost, none of these visitors had previous knowledge of the situation before they arrived, yet several felt the presence of a hostile male. A medium who was invited to investigate but was not told the whereabouts of the presence, experienced the atmosphere as soon as she came in the main door. She felt a weight descend over her and press round her head as she approached the sensitive area A splitting headache prevented her from staying there long yet as soon as she moved away the pressure eased and the pain vanished.

Meanwhile Graham had been experimenting with a pair of divining rods made from copper welding rods. He held the parallel rods loosely in his hands but when he reached the corner of the room they swung violently across each other. The same thing happened in the area directly below.

10: Witchford Aerodrome

During the Spring of 1989 Bill Green of Peterborough was sitting in his car with his wife by the white gate on the left of the bungalow at the edge of former Witchford aerodrome. They had been inspecting the site of the proposed war memorial soon to be erected in memory of No. 115 Squadron, Bomber Command at the head of the wartime runway now returned to farmland. Suddenly he turned to his wife and asked 'Can you see what I am seeing?' She could. They saw… but not clearly… a sensation of people…airmen in uniforms, walking in twos and threes…moving around…looking up at the sky and waving. It was a moonlit evening, six weeks before the memorial was to be erected. There was an impression of traffic coming

Left of the main runway of former Witchford Aerodrome now returned to farmland.

War Memorial erected in memory of No. 115 Squadron, Bomber Command, at Witchford Aerodrome. (top & right).

from the adjacent bypass but also an impression of aircraft engine noise not related to the traffic. After the experience faded a jet aircraft with its navigation lights on, flew at low level over the field.

On July 28th 1996 Chris and Peter Kerswell were looking after the display of wartime memorabilia in the foyer of the Grosvenor building situated on part of the former aerodrome, now the Lancaster Way Business Park. As well as a display of photographs, documents and other artifacts commemorating the Mepal and Witchford airfields there was also an engine from a Lancaster bomber shot down by enemy aircraft and recently dug out of the fen between Ely and Coveney. No. 115 Squadron carried out most raids, flew most sorties and suffered most losses of any Wellington squadron in Bomber Command. They were the only squadron to lose more than 200 aircraft in the war. The Grosvenor building is a new construction of several offices on two levels. As Chris was coming out of the toilet at the rear of the building she heard a loud bang followed by a rumbling sound as though something was being dragged across a stone floor. She thought Peter had decided to move one of the display stands in the tiled foyer and wondered why he hadn't waited for her help. He thought she had fallen over . They hurried towards each other and met in the passageway. All the office doors were locked. Only the toilets were open and they were empty. They both called 'Is anybody there?' but there was no answer. There was nobody else in the building. There was no explanation for the noise. Chris says 'It was a very hot afternoon but my arms were covered with goose bumps and the fine hairs on them stood on end.'

Our tale of Ely ghosts has come full circle. We began at the ancient footpath by Braham Farm where the (7th century) Saxon dog, Black Shuck crosses the A10 towards Witchford Aerodrome. We end at the opposite edge of that same airfield with our most recent sightings from the 20th century. But our tale is never ending. Where there is life there are ghosts.

About the authors

Vivienne Doughty and Margaret Haynes met when they were both teaching in Littleport, a Cambridgeshire village on the edge of the Fens. Neither Vivienne nor Margaret are native to this area but both have come to appreciate and love the mysterious brooding fenland landscape. They both took early retirement and both are developing second careers as Blue Badge Tourist Guides for Ely and East Anglia. Both are fascinated with local history and legends. Margaret specialises in ghost tours while Vivienne concentrates on freelance writing. They decided to pool their resources and begin third careers as authors. Both live in historic old houses but unfortunately neither have met any ghosts.